Is *that* a footprint?

A snowshoe hare
has big feet.
The feet keep the hare
from sinking in the snow.

A snowshoe hare's.

It was made
by running on snow.

Whose footprint is *that?*

A wallaroo can hop
as high as six feet.
It can travel for miles
without getting tired.

A wallaroo's.

These are *two* footprints.
They were made by hopping.

Whose footprint is *that?*

A mountain goat
has rubbery pads
under its toes.
It can climb a rocky cliff
without slipping.

A mountain goat's.

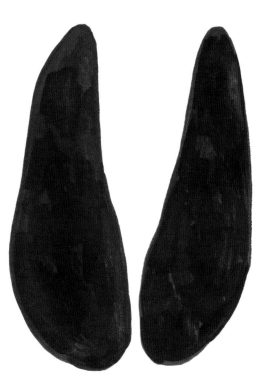

It was made
by two pointy toes.

Whose footprint is *that*?

Whose Footprint
Is THAT?

Darrin Lunde
Illustrated by Kelsey Oseid

ini Charlesbridge

A flamingo's.

It was made by standing
in soft mud.

Whose footprint is *that*?

It was made by a snake.
Snakes don't have feet.
They use their belly muscles
to move.

It was made
by slithering.

That is *not* a footprint.

Flamingos have webbed feet.
The webbing keeps them
from sinking in mud.
A flamingo sleeps
while standing on one leg.

Clunk! Clunk!
Whose footprint is that?

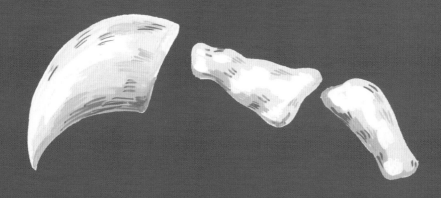

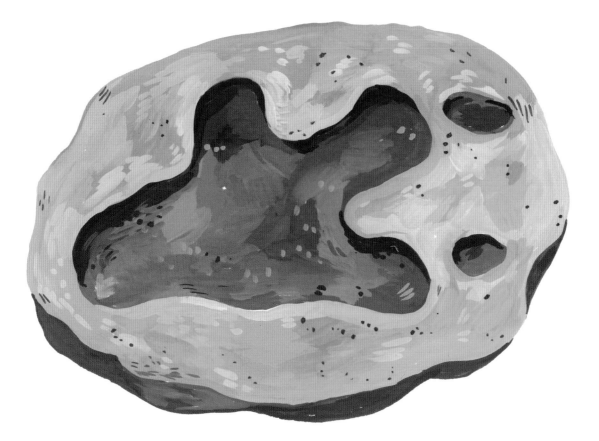

It is a fossil.
It was made long ago.

A dinosaur's.

A dinosaur made its footprints
in soft mud many years ago.
Over time the mud
turned to rock.

Whose footprint is *that*?

It was made
by knuckle walking.

A chimpanzee's.

A chimpanzee stands flat
on its hind feet.
It uses its finger knuckles
for balance when it moves.

Can an animal
change its footprints?

Yes, a human can.

Humans change their footprints by putting things on their feet.

What made each footprint?

For Midori—D. L.
For Declan and Theo and their awesome footprints!—K. O.

Published by Charlesbridge
85 Main Street
Watertown, MA 02472
(617) 926-0329
www.charlesbridge.com

Library of Congress Cataloging-in-Publication Data
Names: Lunde, Darrin P., author. | Oseid, Kelsey, illustrator.
Title: Whose footprint is that? / Darrin Lunde; illustrated by Kelsey Oseid.
Description: Watertown, MA: Charlesbridge, [2019]
Identifiers: LCCN 2018032577 (print) | LCCN 2018036843 (ebook) |
    ISBN 9781632897213 (ebook) | ISBN 9781632897220 (ebook pdf) |
    ISBN 9781580898348 (reinforced for library use)
Subjects: LCSH: Animal tracks—Juvenile literature. | Animal locomotion—Juvenile literature.
Classification: LCC QL768 (ebook) | LCC QL768 .L85 2019 (print) |
    DDC 591.47/9—dc23
LC record available at https://lccn.loc.gov/2018032577

Printed in China
(hc) 10 9 8 7 6 5 4 3 2 1

Illustrations done with gouache on paper
Display type set in Graphen by Maciej Wloczewski
Text type set in Franklin Gothic Hand Light by Gert Wiescher, Wiescher-Design
Color separations by Colourscan Print Co Pte Ltd, Singapore
Printed by 1010 Printing International Limited in Huizhou, Guangdong, China
Production supervision by Brian G. Walker
Designed by Sarah Richards Taylor